BIRDS

Animal Group Science Book For Kids
Children's Zoology Books Edition

Speedy Publishing LLC
40 E. Main St. #1156
Newark, DE 19711
www.speedypublishing.com

Birds are characterised by feathers, a beak with no teeth, the laying of hard-shelled eggs, a four-chambered heart, and a lightweight but strong skeleton.

Hummingbirds are among the smallest of birds. The hummingbird can hover, fly forwards, backwards and even upside down.

They are called hummingbirds due to the sound created by their rapidly beating wings. They have feet so tiny that they cannot walk on the ground.

Owls are birds of prey. Owls are active at night. Most owls hunt insects, small mammals and other birds.

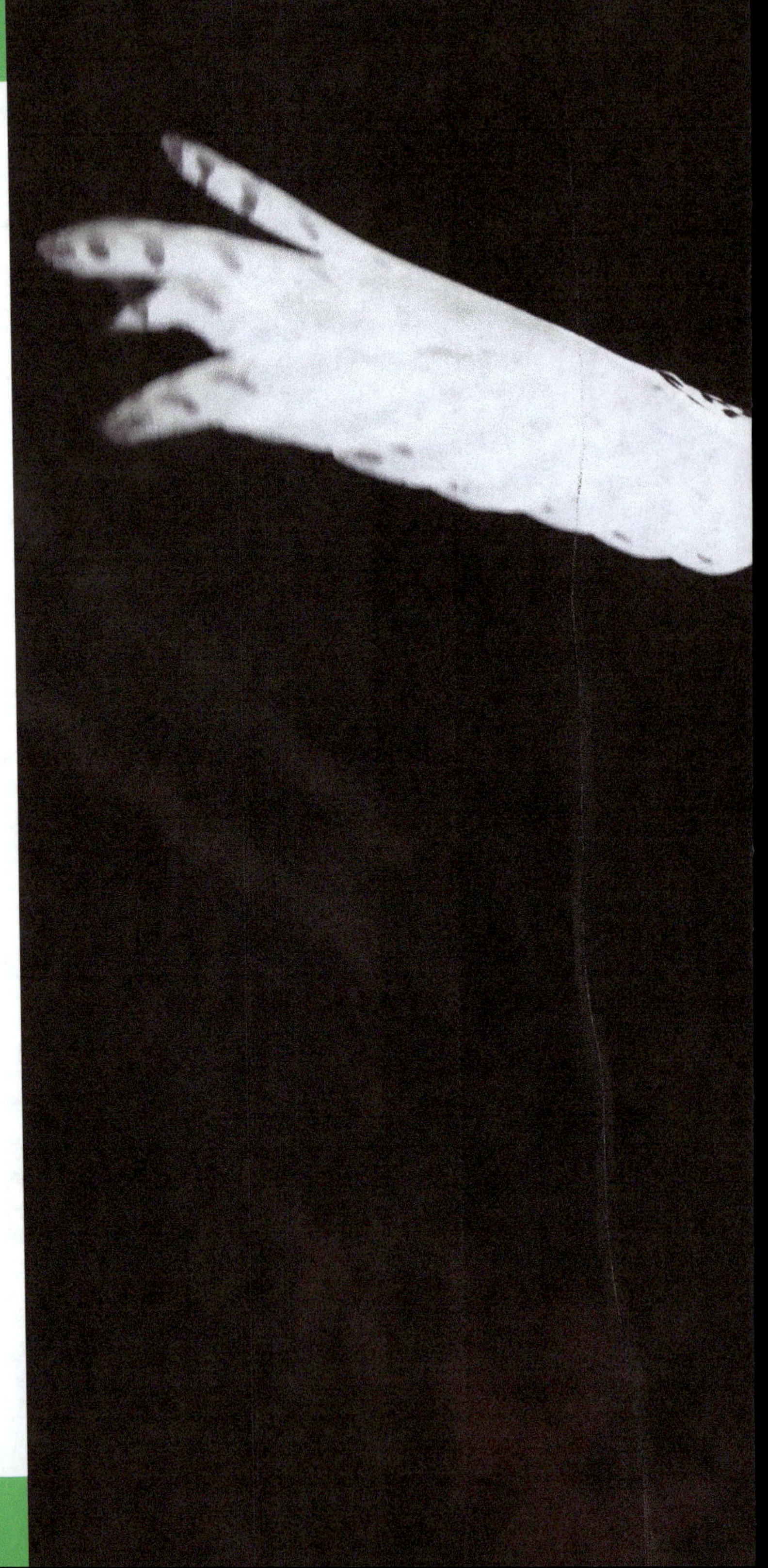

Owls can turn their heads almost completely around. Owls are farsighted, meaning they can't see things close to their eyes clearly.

Penguins are a group of aquatic, flightless birds living almost exclusively in the Southern Hemisphere.

Penguins spend around half their time in water and the other half on land. Penguins have excellent eyesight and hearing.

The ostrich is the largest living species of bird. They also lay the largest eggs of any living bird.

Ostriches live in the African savannah. They can run up to 43 miles per hour for short periods.

Toucans are renown for their large colorful bills. Toucans reside in the jungles of South America and Central America.

Toucans mainly eat fruit, but sometimes prey on insects and small lizards.

A cockatoo are recognisable by the showy crests and curved bills. Cockatoos prefer to eat seeds, tubers, corms, fruit, flowers and insects.

Cockatoos are very smart, but if they get bored, they sometimes destroy things.

The peregrine falcon is perhaps best identified by the black mask of feathers that covers its face.

The peregrine is renowned for its speed, reaching over 322 kilometers per hour.

Flamingos live in areas of large shallow lakes, lagoons, mangrove swamps, tidal flats, and sandy islands.

Flamingos have a funny way of eating. They place their bills upside down in the water and suck water into their mouths.

Vultures
are nature's
garbage men.
Vultures eat
animals that
have died in
the wild.

Vultures have excellent senses of sight and smell to help them locate food, and they can find a dead animal from a mile or more away.

www.ingramcontent.com/pod-product-compliance
Lightning Source LLC
LaVergne TN
LVHW060830170826
845678LV00010B/1948
9798869449160